PJ MASKS

Coloring Book

Copyright © 2019 All rights reserved. No part of this publication may be reproduced, distributed, or transmitted in any form or by any means, including photocopying, recording, electronic or mechanical methods, without the prior written permission of the publisher, except in the case of brief quotations in critical reviews and certain other noncommercial uses permitted by copyright law.

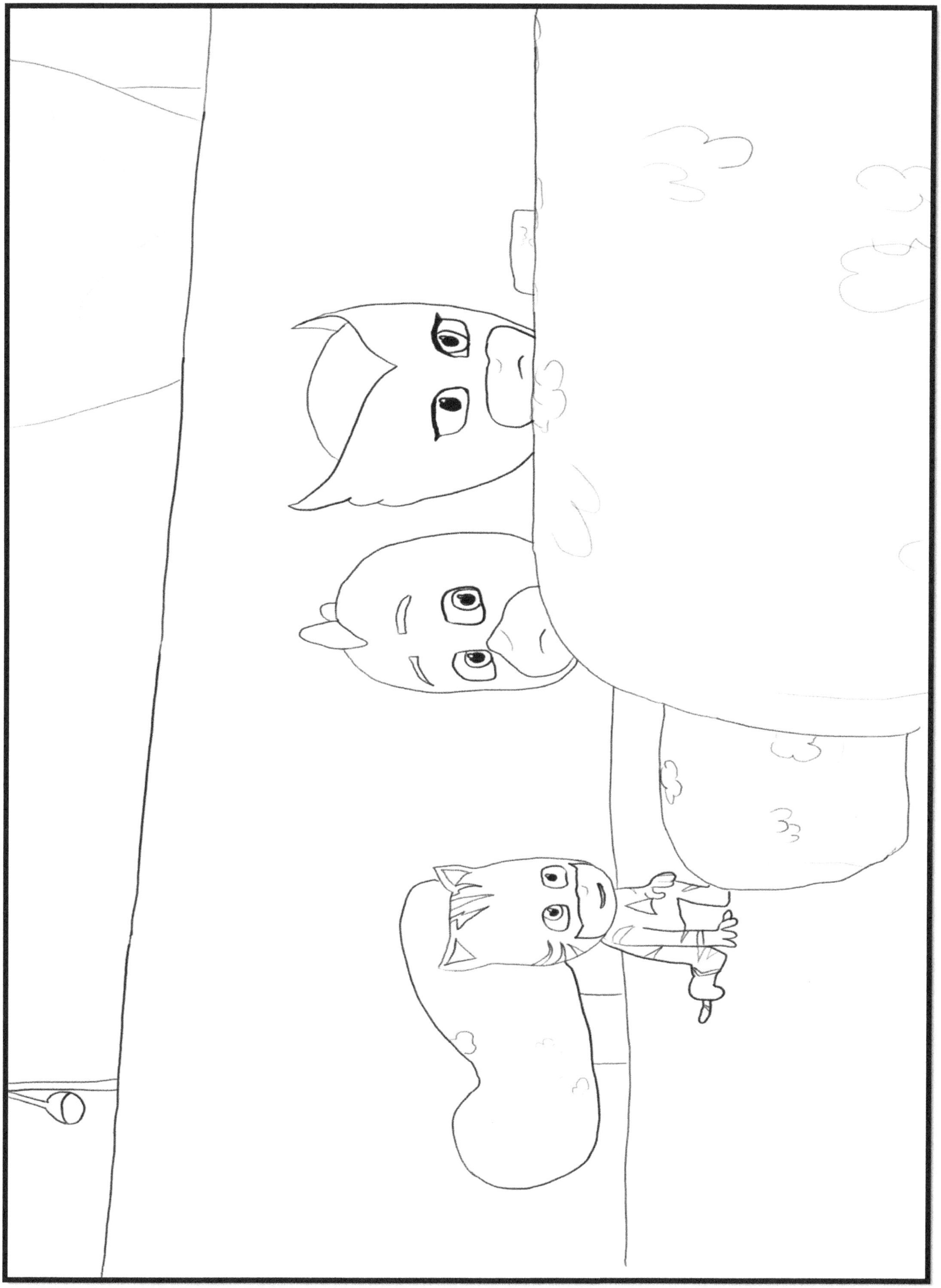

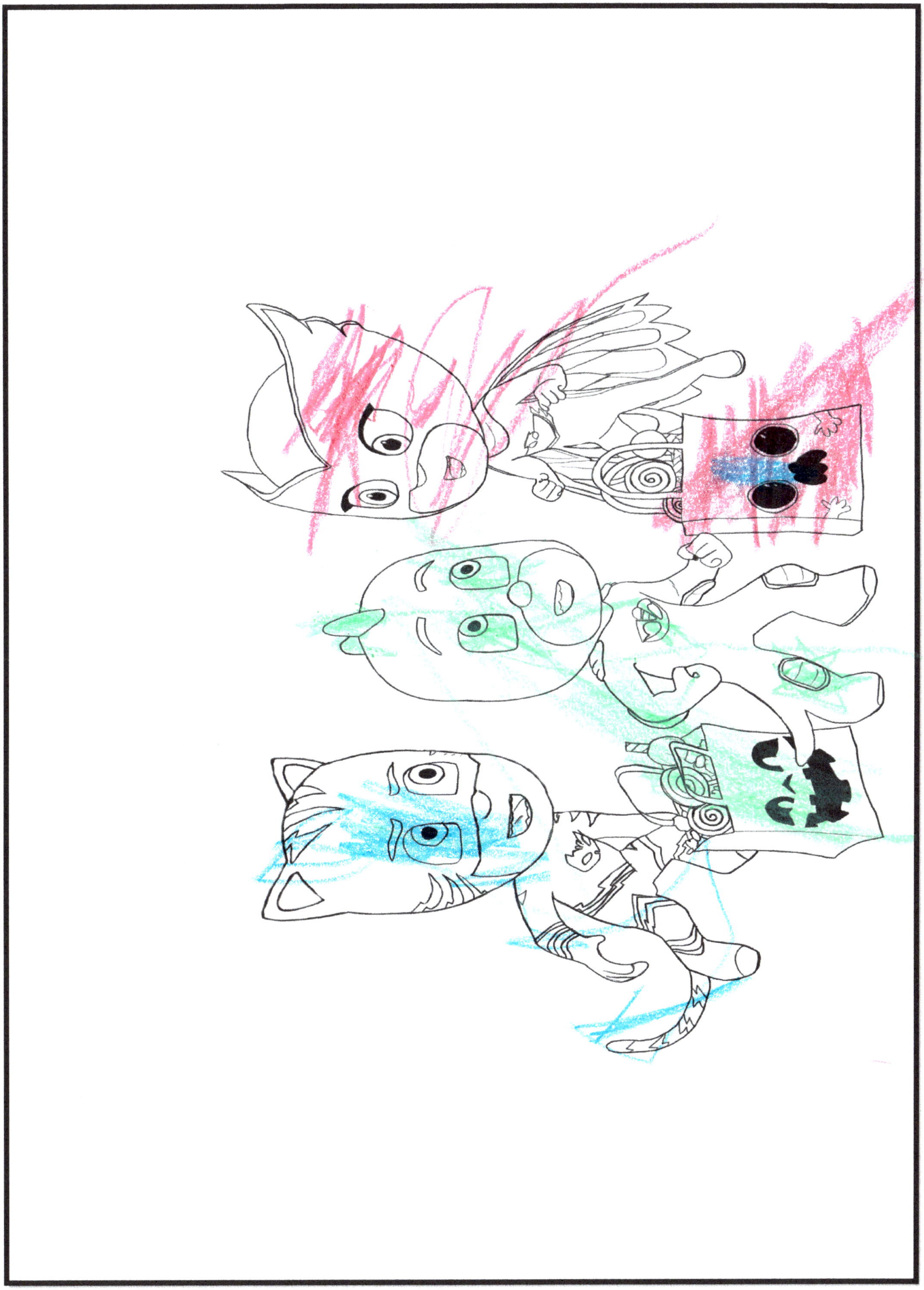

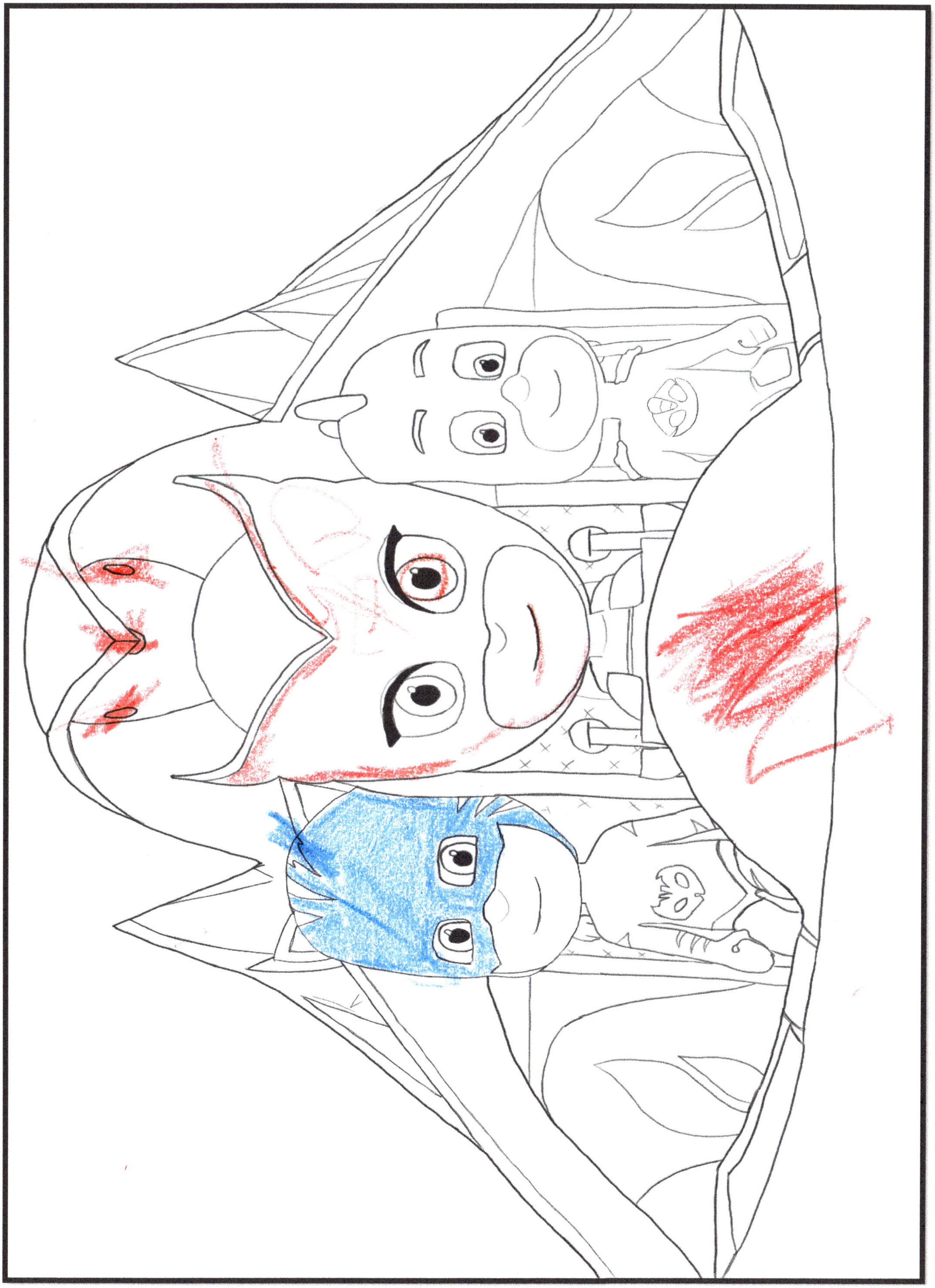

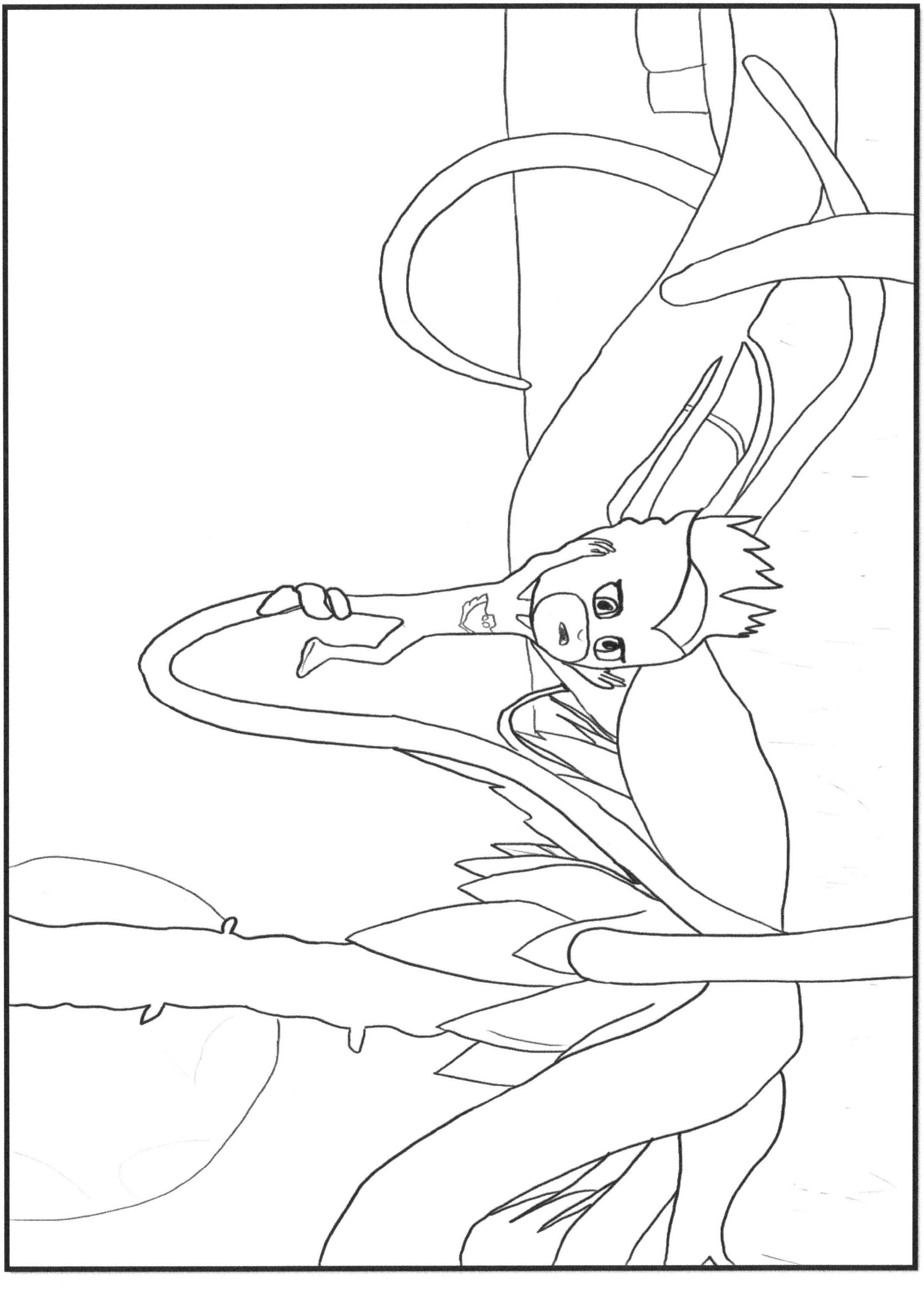

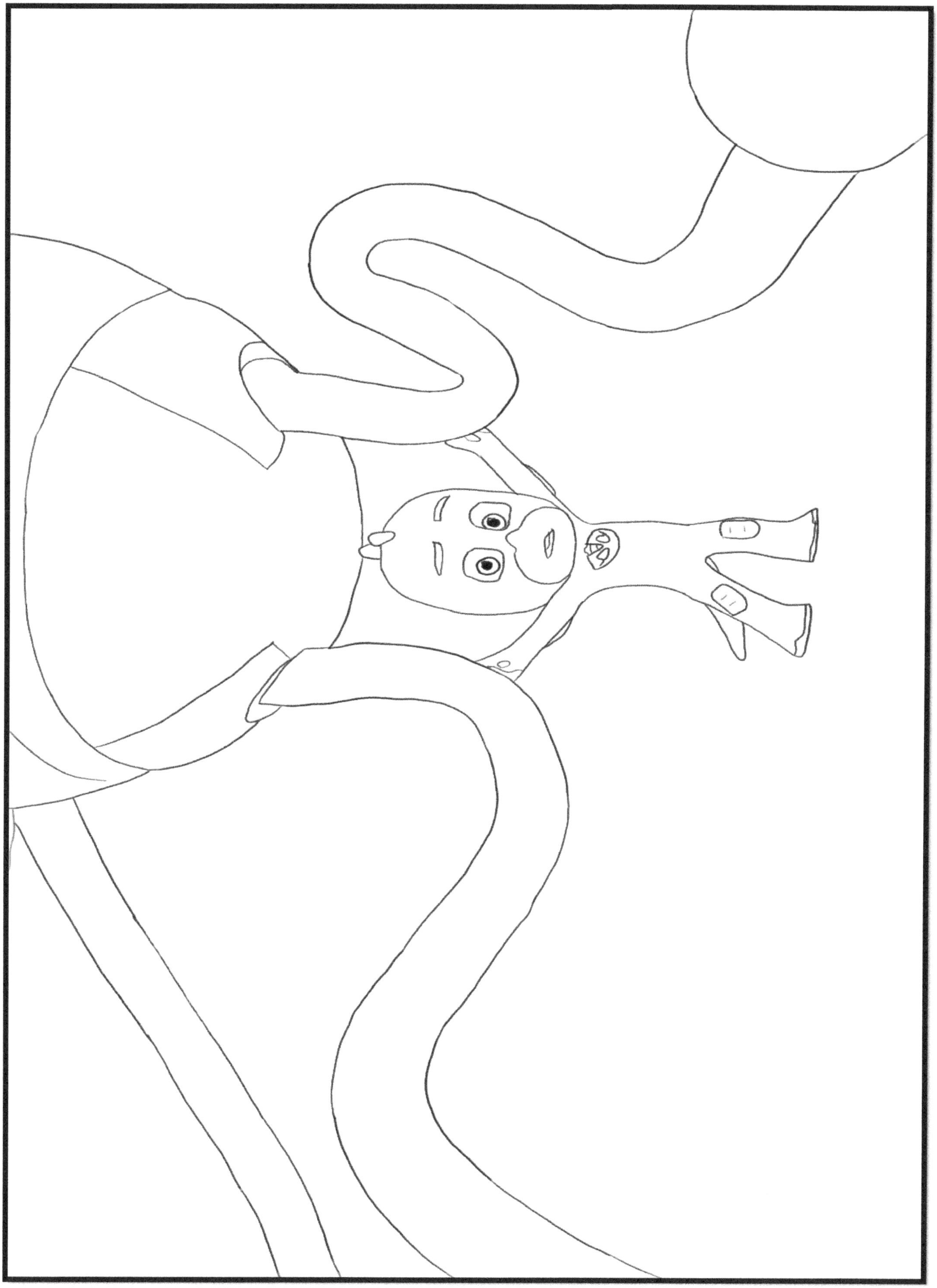

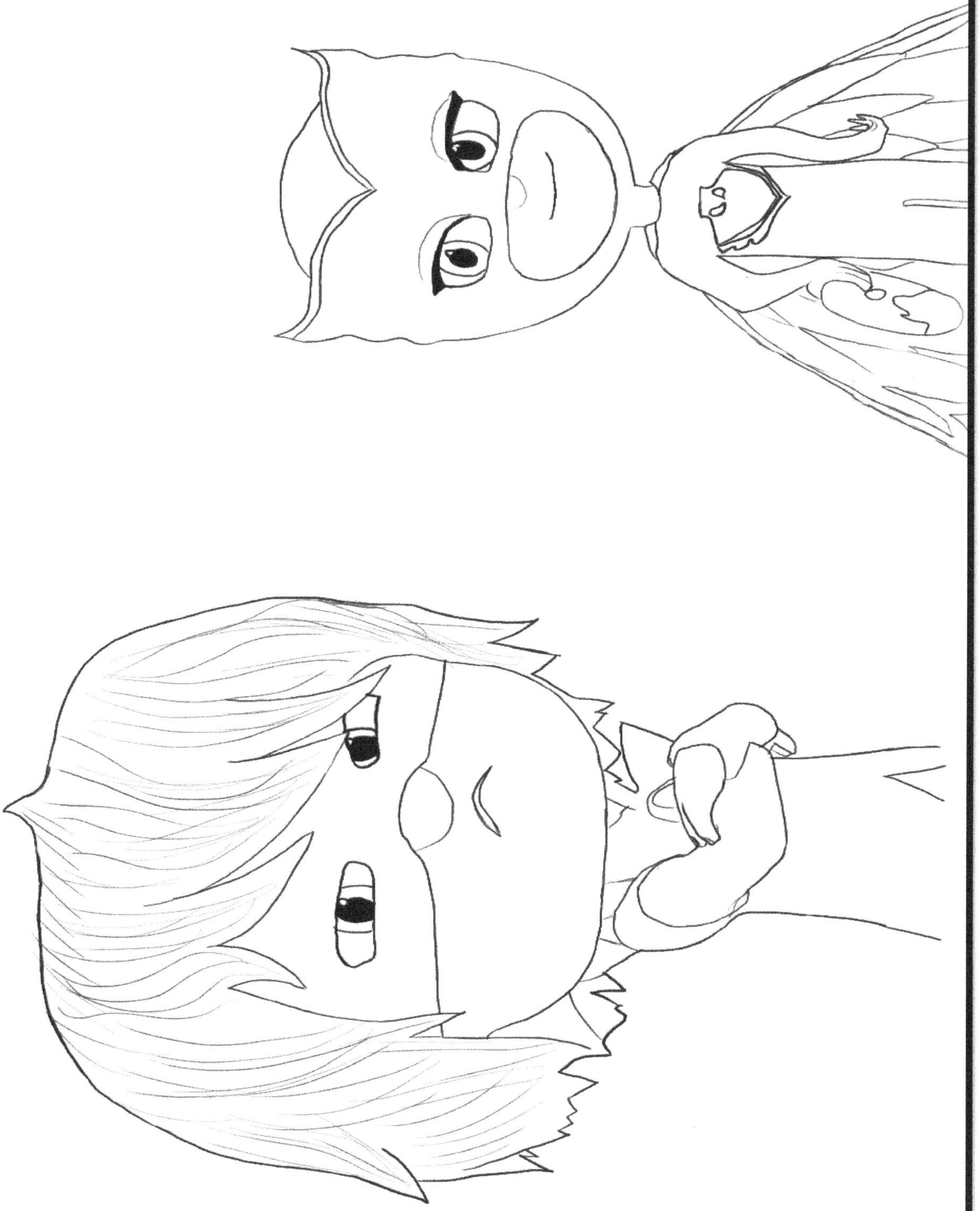

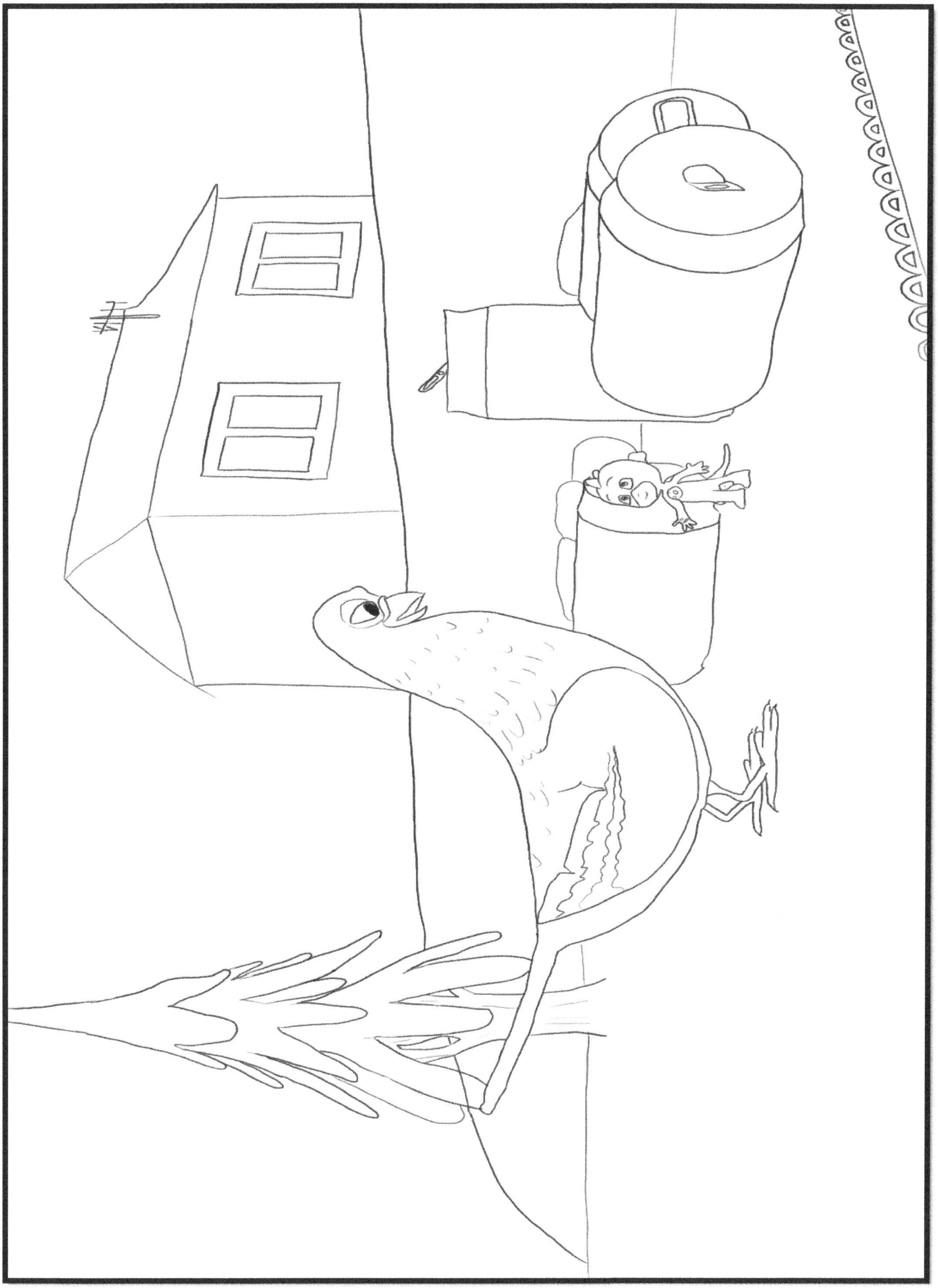

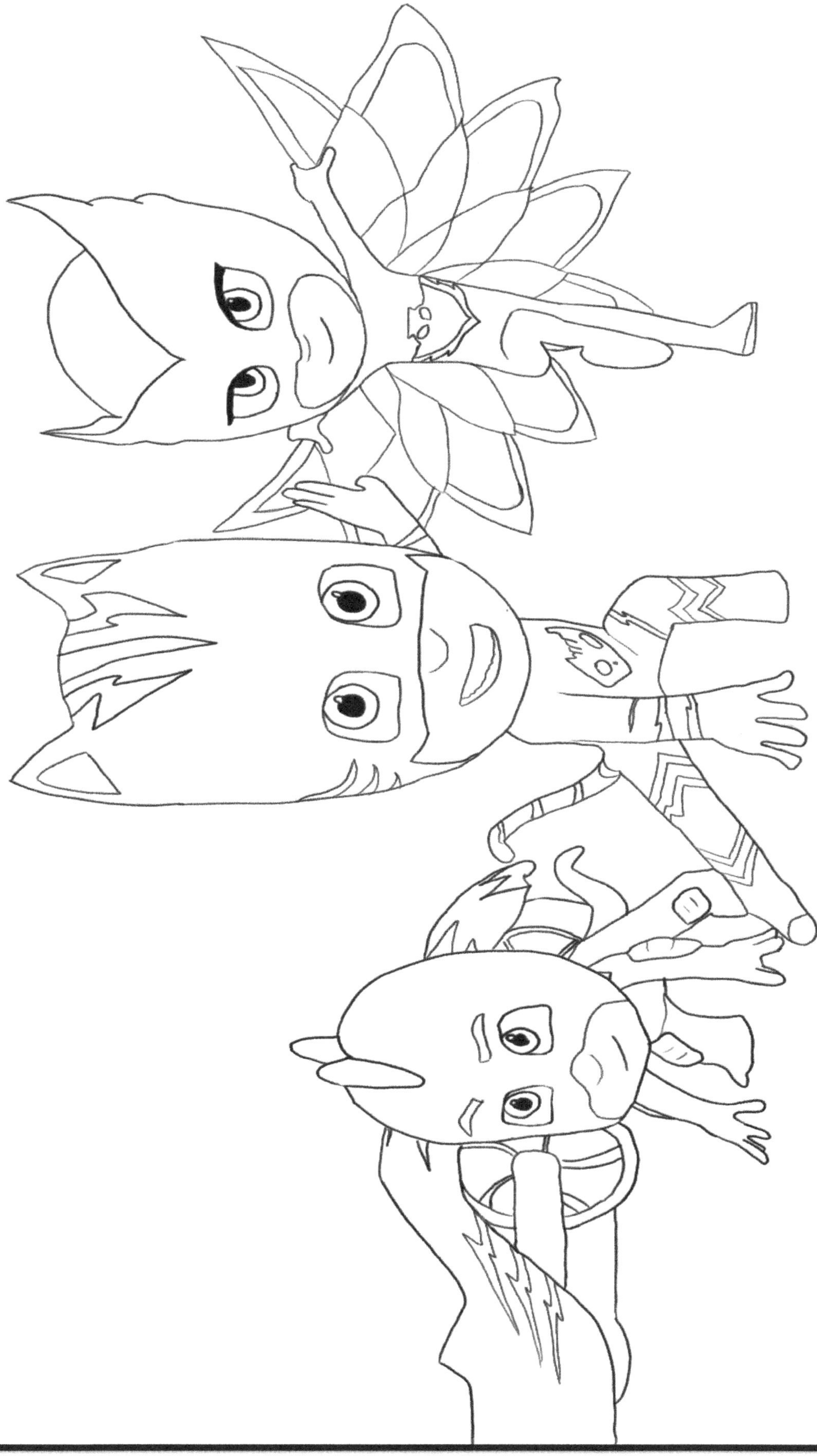

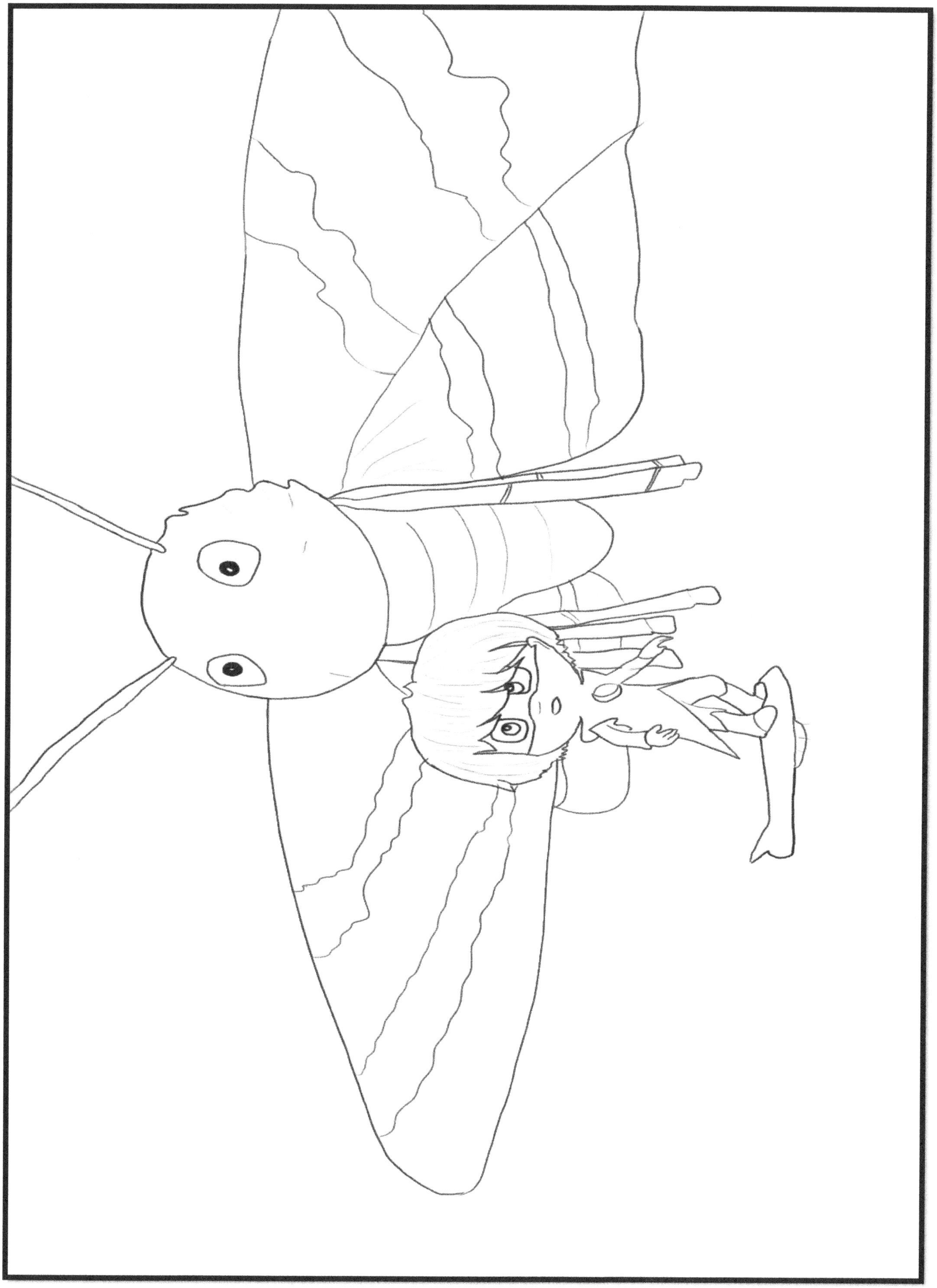

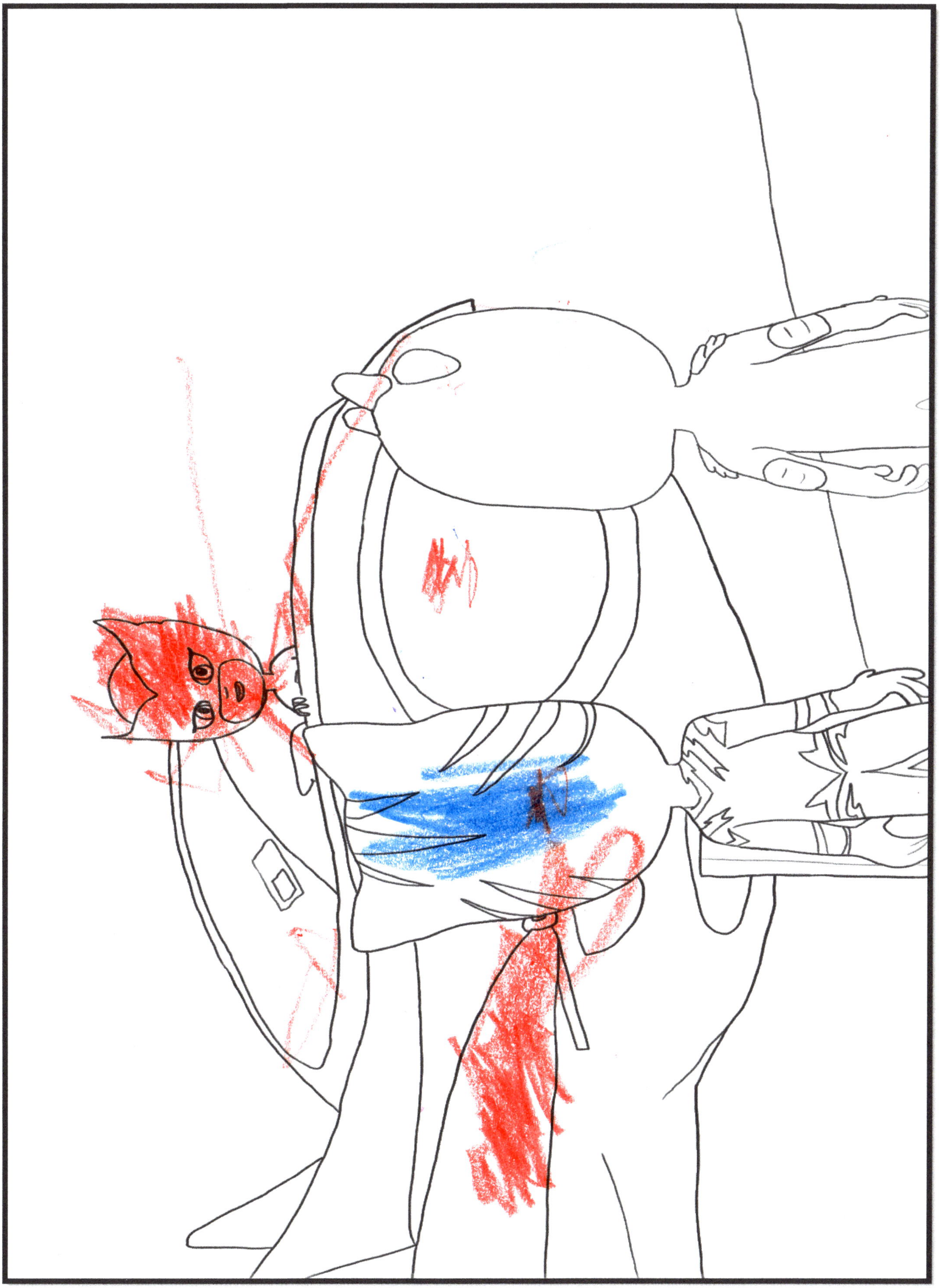

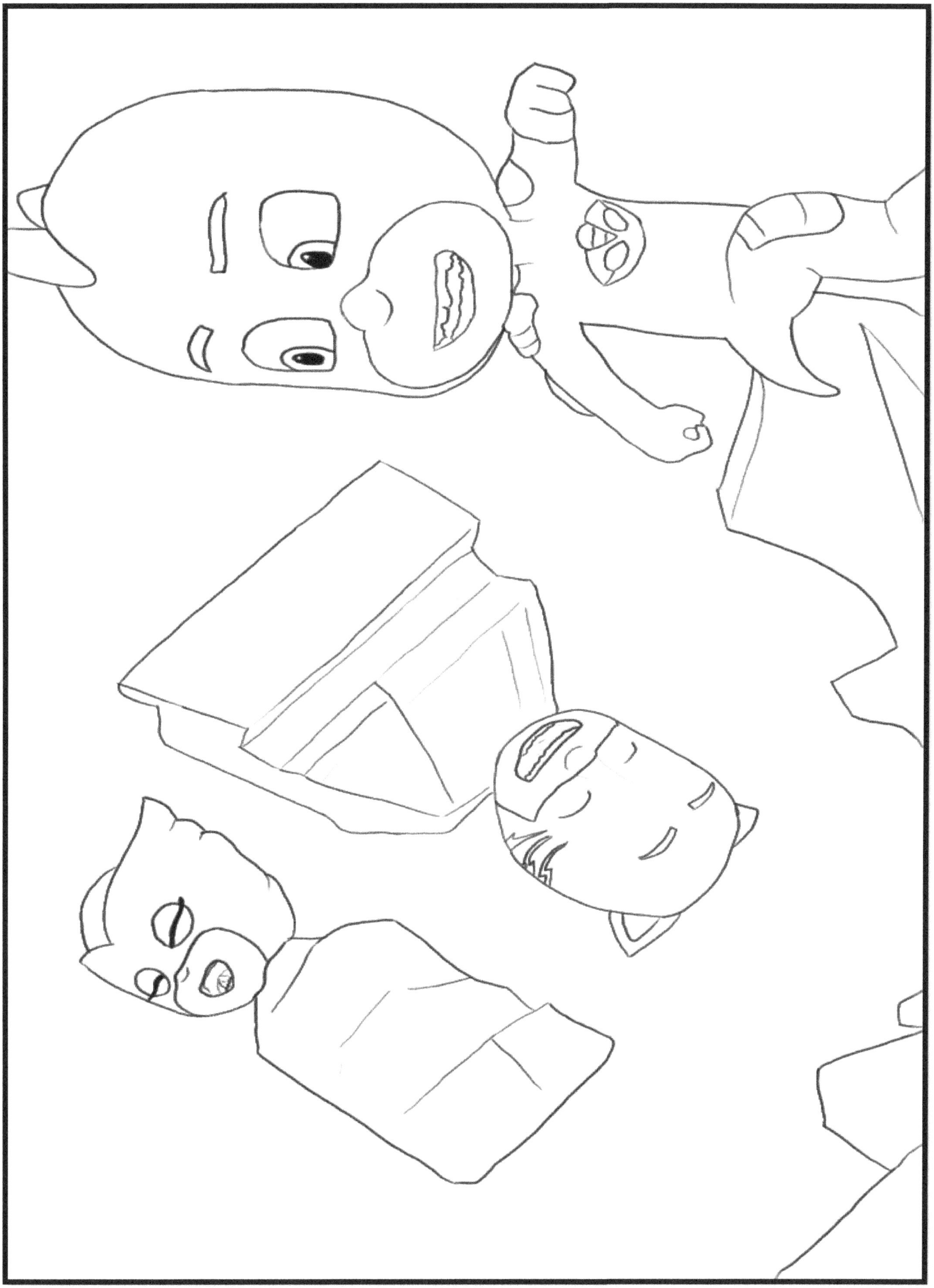

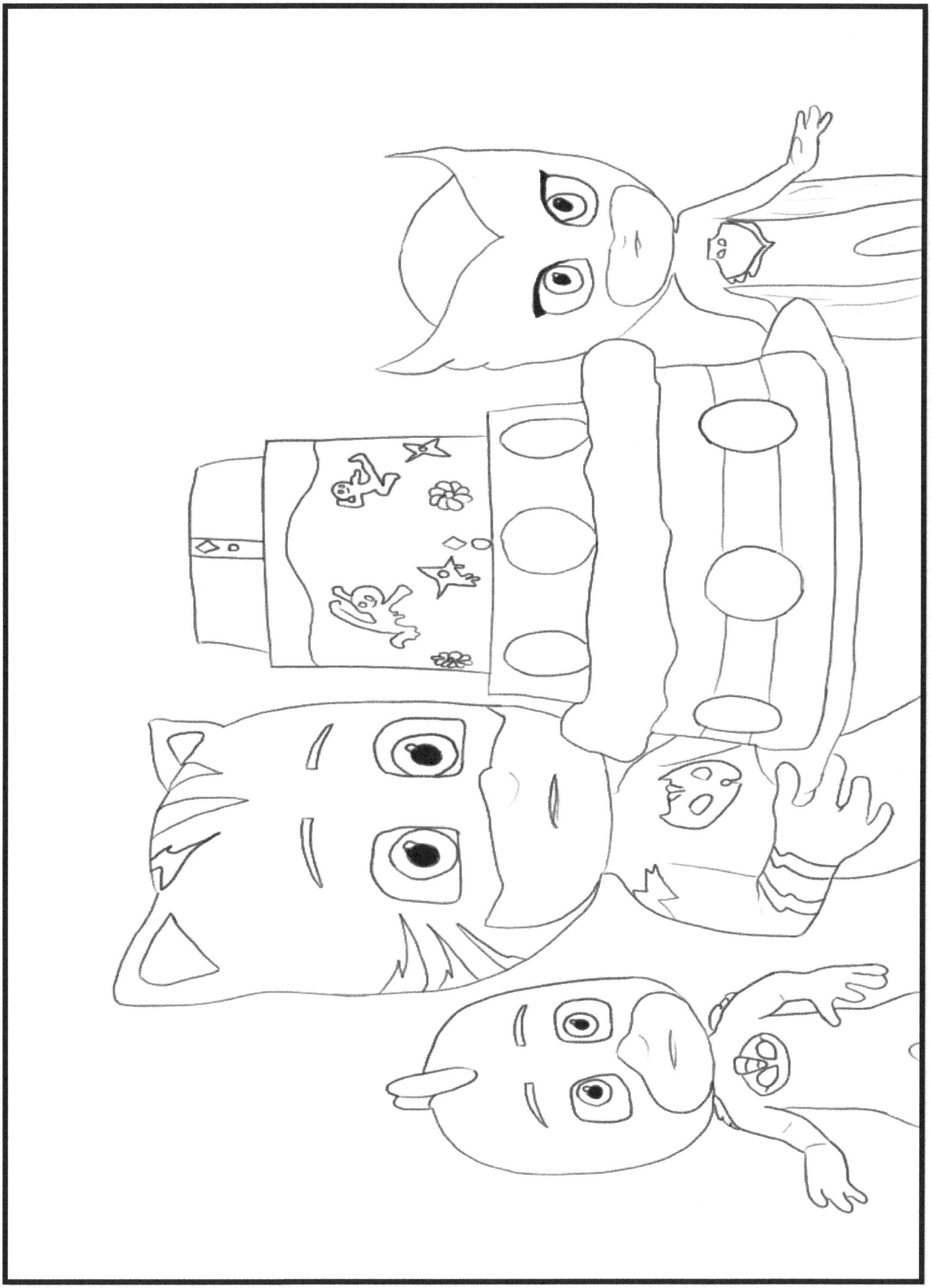

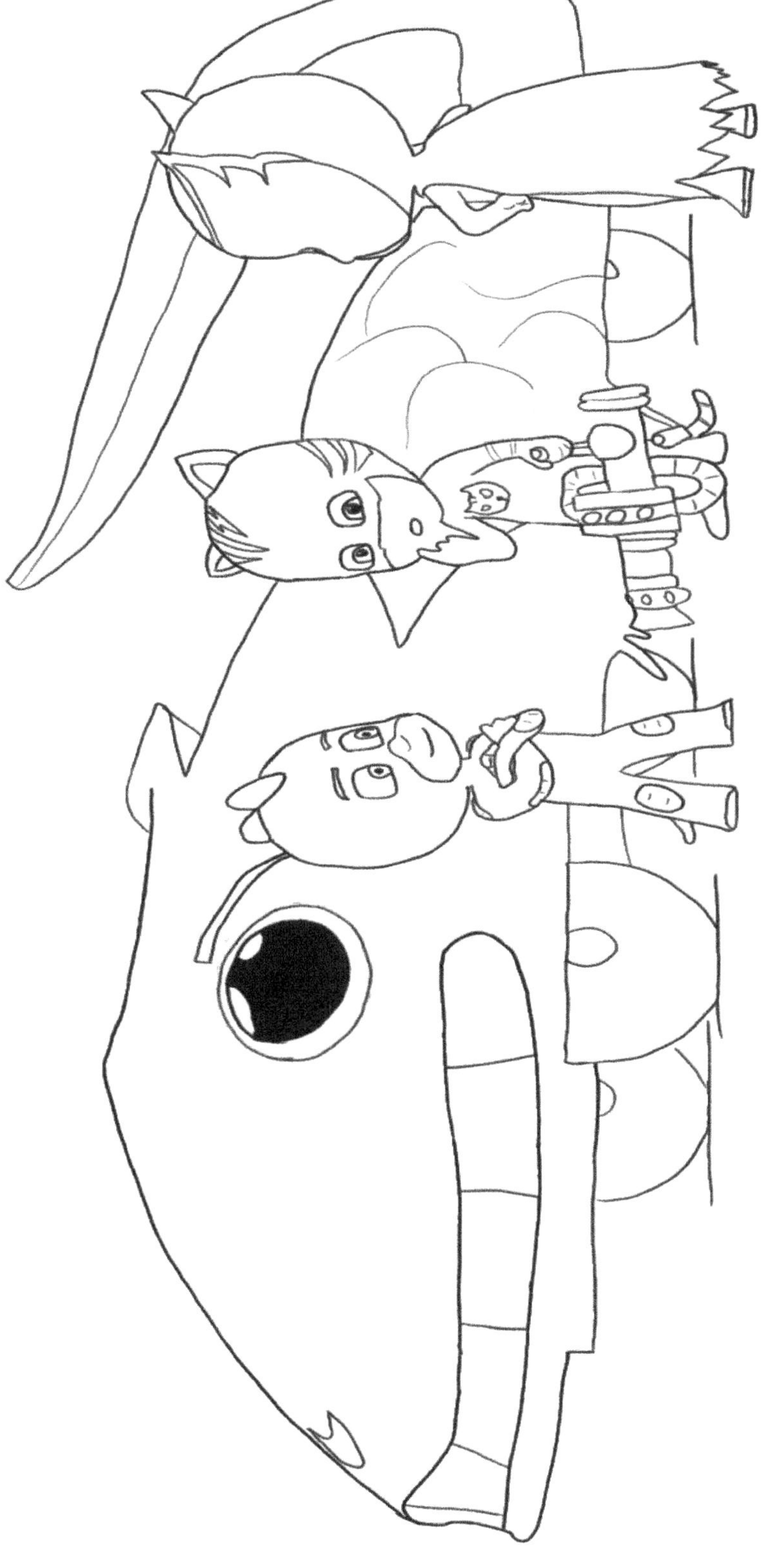

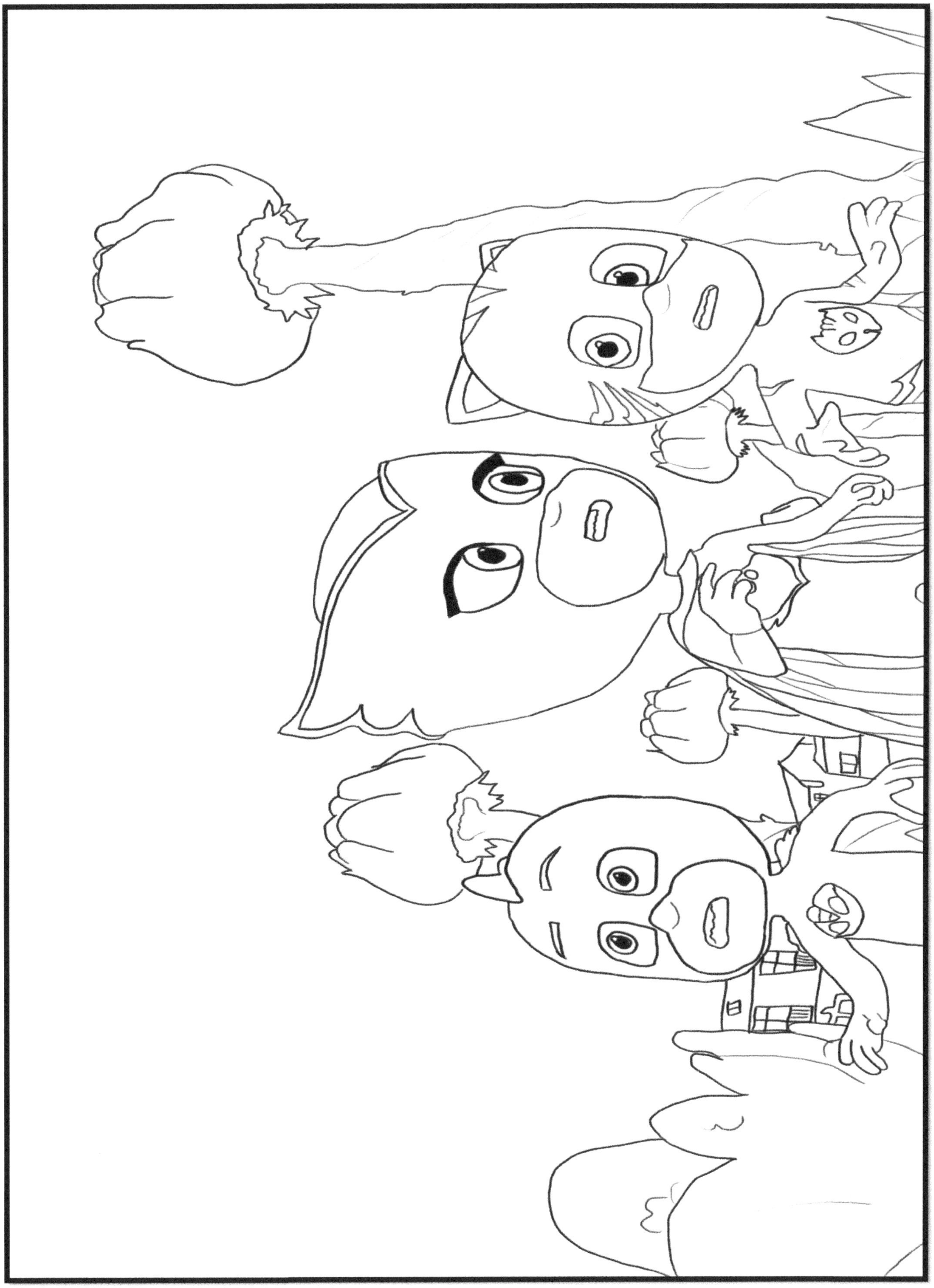

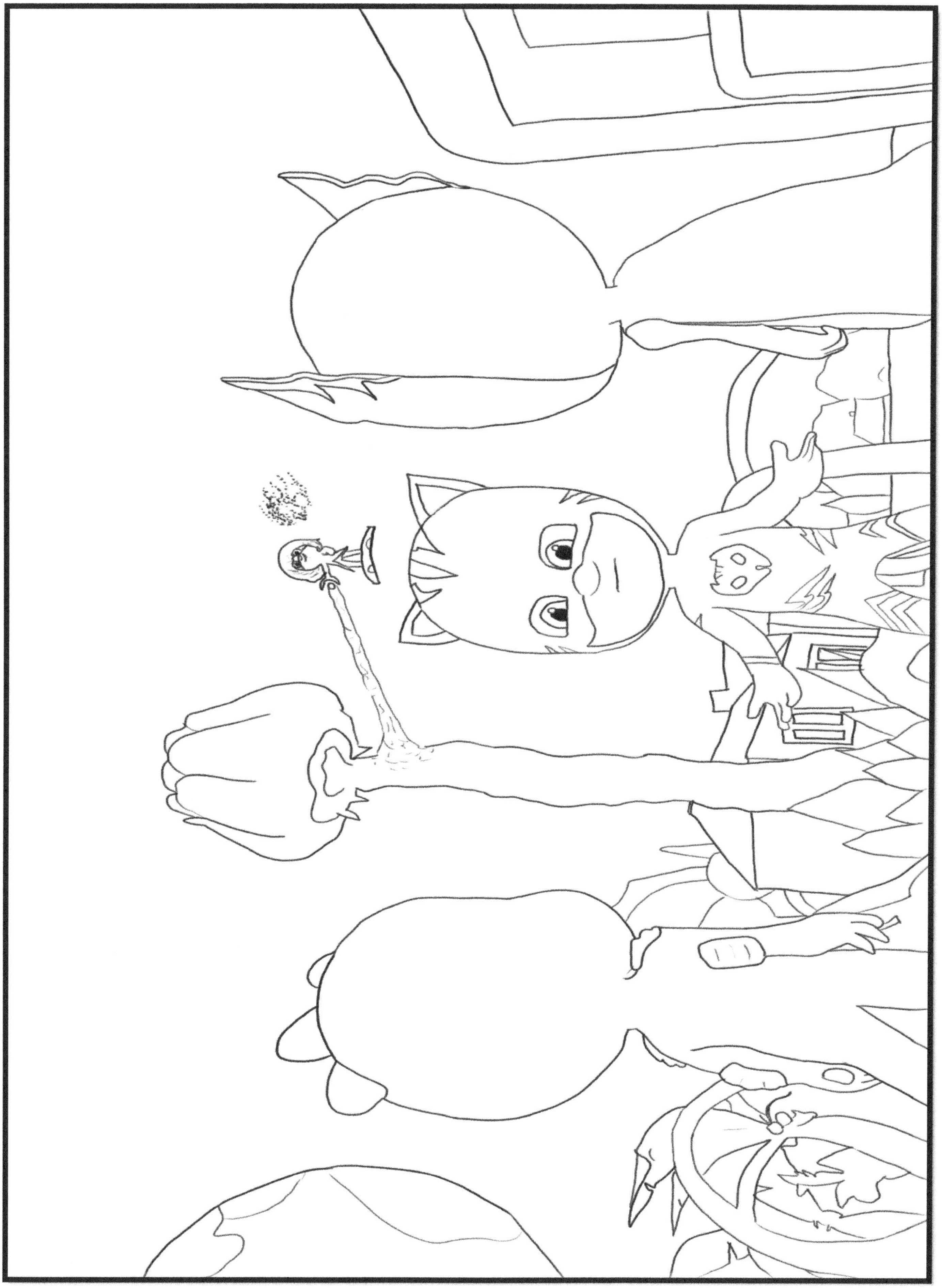

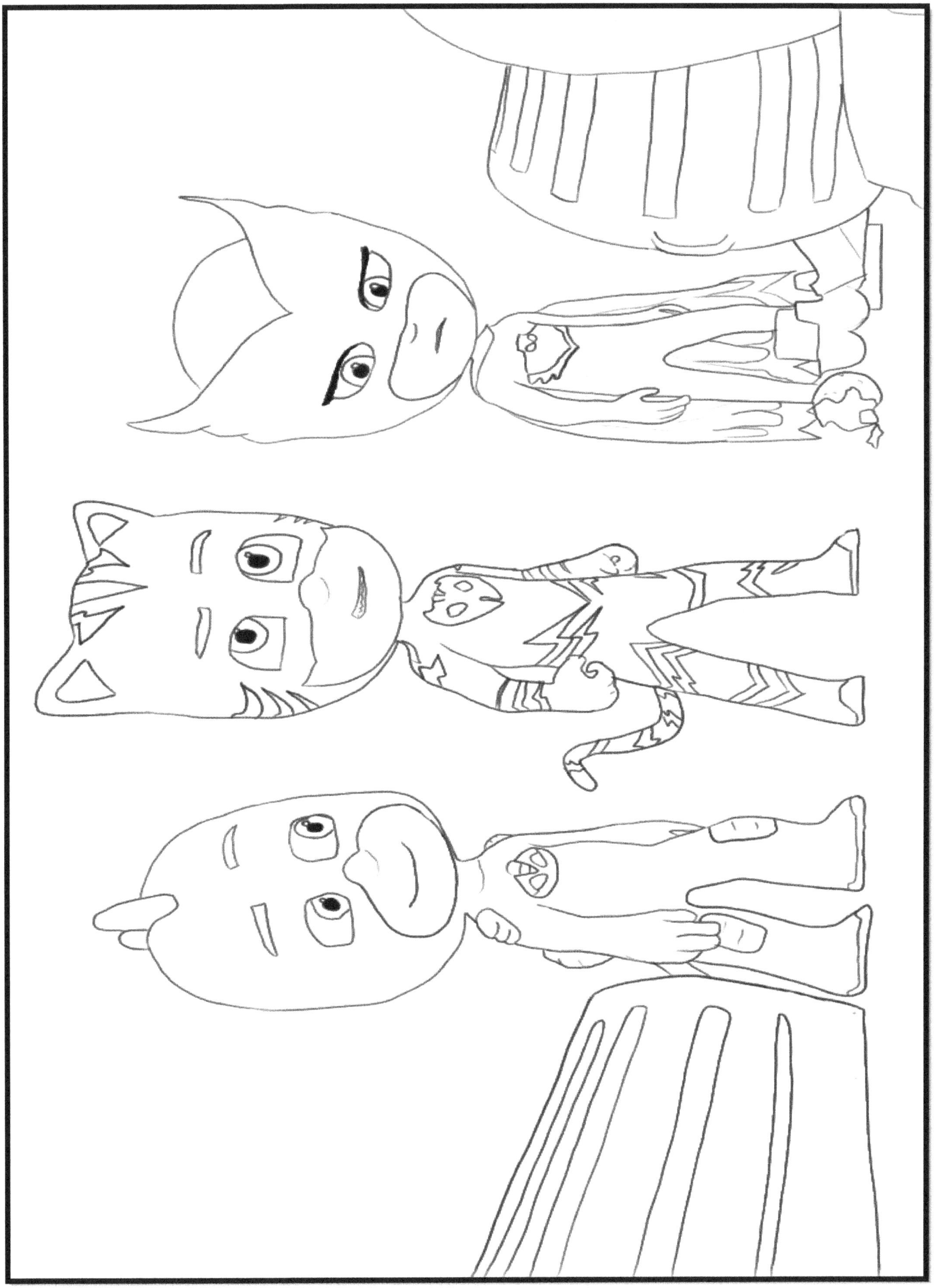

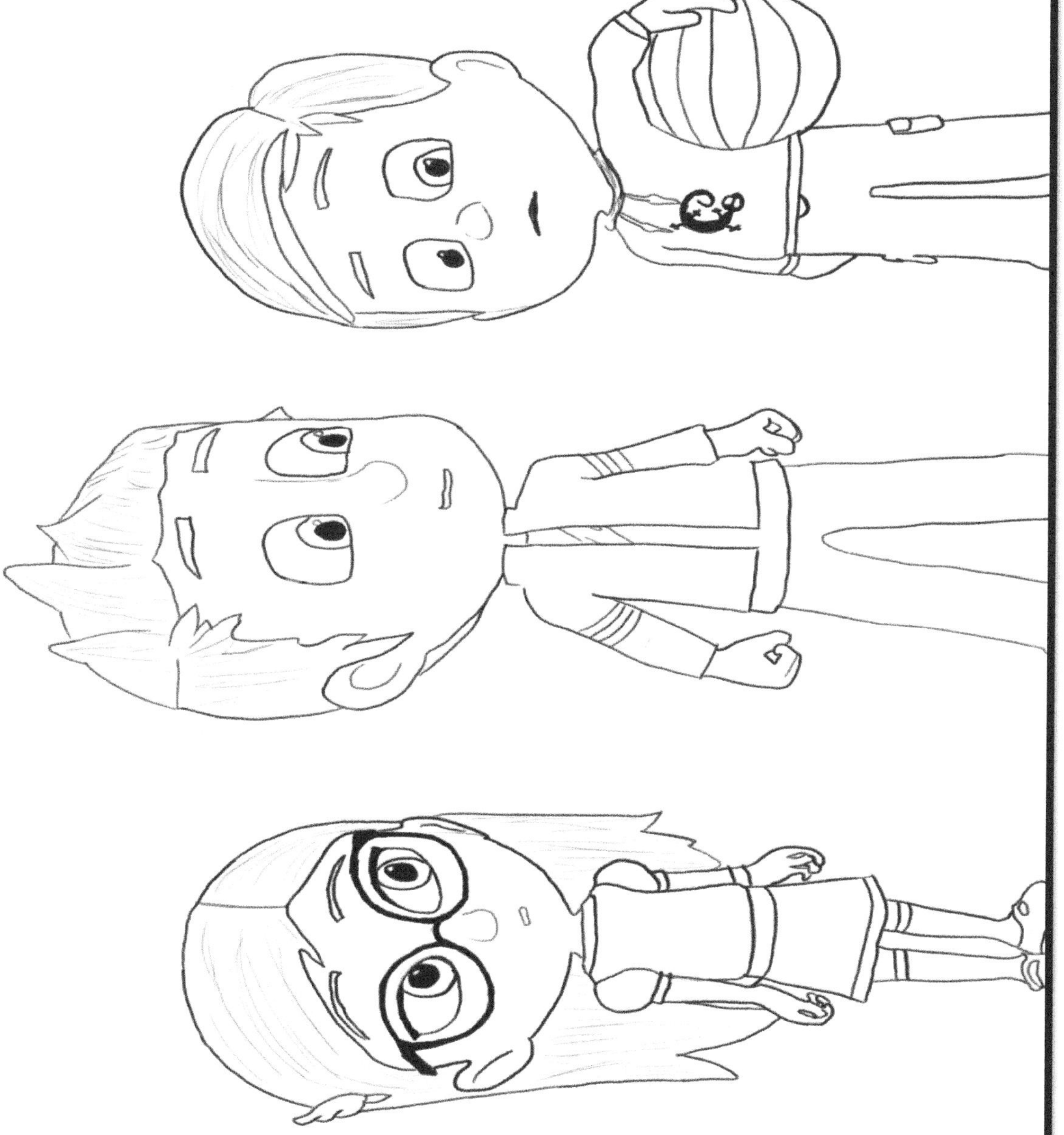

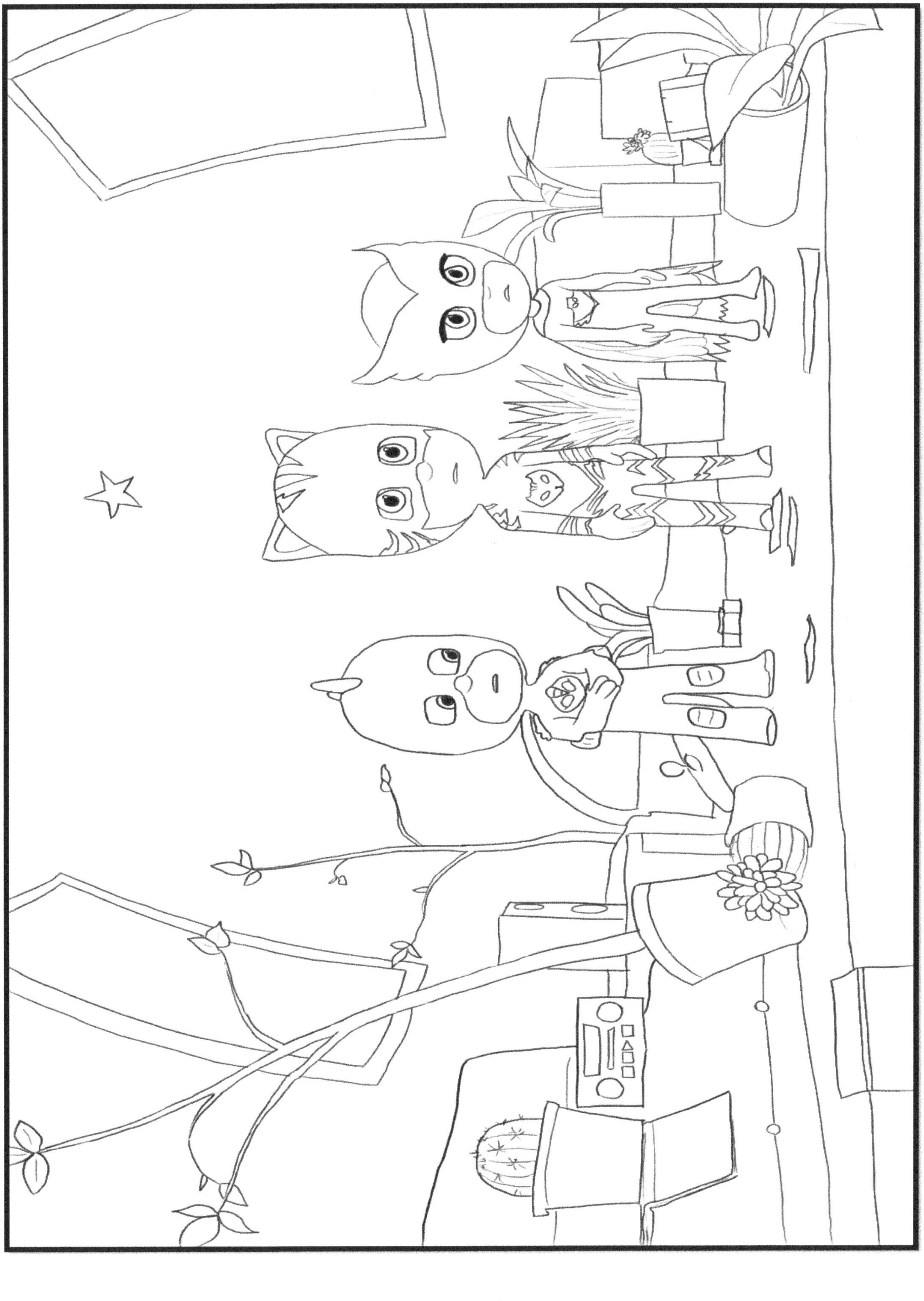

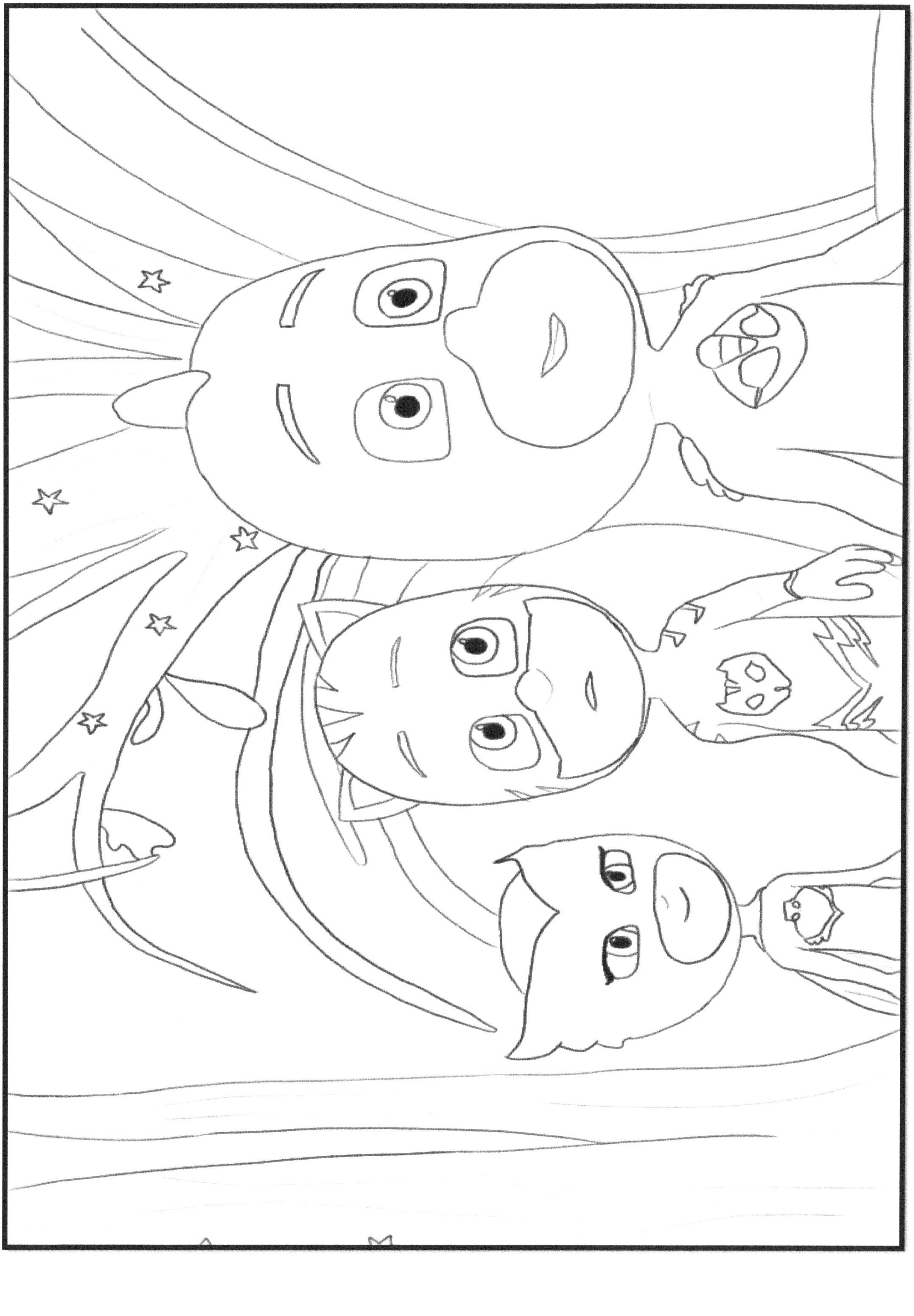

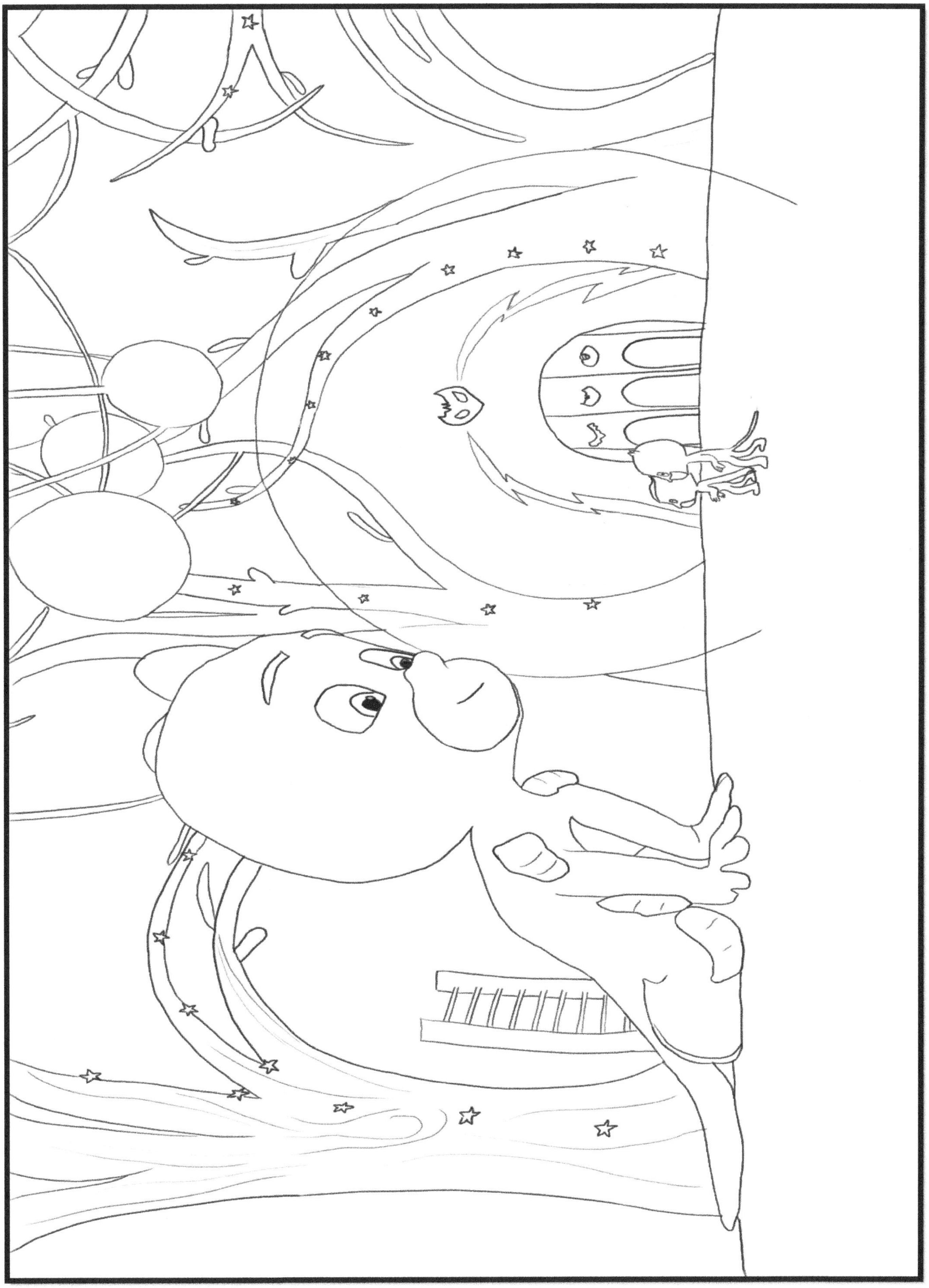

Made in the USA
Monee, IL
22 December 2019